THERE YET?

beep
beep

ISBN-13: 978-1-56383-654-1
Item #2923

Printed in the USA

Distributed By:

PO Box 850
Waverly, IA 50677

www.cqbookstore.com

gifts@cqbookstore.com

 CQ Products

 CQ Products

 @cqproducts

 @cqproducts

Hey RVers...

When you hit the road, you pack your gear, you pack your supplies, you pack your necessities... just don't forget to pack this great cookbook! It's the tool you need to ensure an enjoyable trip without worrying about what to cook.

The meals inside are big on taste but short on the time it takes to make them.

Go enjoy yourself! And leave the cooking ideas to us.

Your Traveling Food Tips:

- Plan meals ahead of time.
- Make a master grocery list.
- Take limited fresh food; buy more later.
- Canned food travels well (don't forget a can opener).
- Shop local farmers' markets when possible.
- Eat well every day.

Fluffy Flapjacks

5 eggs

2 C. pancake mix

2 T. sugar

½ tsp. cinnamon

2 T. melted butter

½ C. 7-Up or Sprite

Butter and maple syrup
for serving

In a bowl, whisk the eggs until well beaten. Add the pancake mix, sugar, and cinnamon. Pour in the butter and 7-Up or Sprite. Stir until just combined *(the mixture will be lumpy).*

Heat a griddle or skillet and spritz with cooking spray. Pour the batter onto the hot pan using about ⅓ cup for each pancake. Cook until golden brown on both sides, flipping once.

Serve with butter and maple syrup.

Carbonation is the secret to these fluffy pancakes. You could also try using ginger beer (which is nonalcoholic) or seltzer water for a different twist.

Bacon-Corn Dip

6 strips bacon, chopped

3 C. corn kernels (thawed if frozen; drained if canned)

½ C. diced onion

¼ C. diced red bell pepper

1 jalapeño, seeded & diced

4 oz. cream cheese, cut into small cubes

¼ C. sour cream

2 green onions, thinly sliced

1 tsp. sugar

¼ tsp. salt

½ tsp. black pepper

Crackers and/or tortilla chips for serving

Cook bacon until brown and crispy. Transfer to a paper towel-lined plate to drain; set aside until cool.

In a mixing bowl, combine the corn, onion, bell pepper, jalapeño, cream cheese, sour cream, green onions, sugar, salt, black pepper, and cooked bacon. Refrigerate for at least 1 hour before serving. Serve with crackers or tortilla chips. **Serves 8**

Zesty Shrimp & Rice

Heat oven to 425°. Dump 2 (10 oz.) pkgs. frozen rice & vegetable blend *(we used a blend of brown and wild rice with corn, carrots, and peas)* into a greased 9 x 13" pan. Add 1½ lbs. raw shrimp *(peeled & deveined)* and 1 lemon *(cut into wedges)*.

Mix 1 (.7 oz.) pkg. dry Italian salad dressing mix with ½ C. melted butter and pour over the food in the pan; stir to coat. Cover and bake for 30 minutes, until the shrimp turn pink, stirring once during baking.

Make it oven-free: *Heat in a skillet over medium-low heat, until shrimp turn pink.*

7

Serves 4

Alfredo Bacon Pizza

1 (13.8 oz.) tube refrigerated pizza crust dough

1 C. bacon flavored or plain Alfredo sauce

1¼ C. shredded mozzarella cheese, divided

1 (10 oz.) pkg. frozen chopped spinach, thawed, drained & squeezed dry

2 or 3 plum tomatoes, thinly sliced

5 precooked bacon strips

Heat oven to 425°. Coat a 12" pizza pan with cooking spray.

Unroll the dough and press evenly into the prepped pan, making a small rim around outer edge. Spread the sauce over the dough and sprinkle with ½ cup of the cheese. Arrange the spinach and tomatoes over the cheese. Cut the bacon strips into 1" pieces and arrange over the top; sprinkle the remaining ¾ cup cheese over all.

Bake for 15 minutes or until the crust is golden brown and the cheese is melted.

Make it oven-free: *Use flatbread instead of pizza dough, preheat your grill to medium-high heat, cover grates with greased foil, and grill the pizza until the cheese melts.*

Berry-licious French Toast

1 (1 lb.) loaf sliced
   cinnamon-raisin bread

6 eggs

1 tsp. vanilla

⅓ C. milk

¾ C. heavy cream, divided

2 T. pure maple syrup, plus
   more for serving

1 to 1½ C. fresh blueberries
   and/or raspberries

1 C. powdered sugar

Heat oven to 375°. Lay two big sheets of heavy-duty foil on top of each other on a rimmed baking sheet and spritz with cooking spray. Set the loaf of bread in the center of the foil; fold the edges up around the bottom half of the loaf to hold the bread in place and keep the egg mixture contained. Fan out the bread slices slightly.

In a bowl, beat the eggs. Whisk in the vanilla, milk, ½ cup of the cream, and 2 tablespoons of the maple syrup. Pour the mixture slowly over the top of the bread, making sure to soak both sides of each slice. Scatter the berries over the top, pushing some between the slices. Cover the bread with another big sheet of foil; crimp the edges to seal the bread inside. Bake for 30 to 45 minutes, until the eggs are set, removing the top foil during the last 10 minutes if necessary to prevent overbrowning.

Mix the powdered sugar with enough of the remaining cream to make a drizzling consistency. Open the foil and drizzle the glaze over the bread. Serve with maple syrup.

Wide-Eyed Cold Brew

The night before, put ½ C. ground coffee into a 1-quart mason jar; fill the jar with water, cover, and let set overnight at room temperature.

The next morning, strain through cheesecloth into a clean mason jar; discard coffee grounds. Add water to the coffee to fill the jar.

To serve, fill a 1-pint jar with ice; fill ⅔ full with the coffee. Add a big splash of half & half and sweetened condensed milk to taste. Stir before serving. **Serves 8**

Maple-Orange Squash

Preheat your grill to medium heat. Manwhile peel, seed & cut 1 lb. butternut squash into 1" cubes and microwave for 2 minutes *(or par-cook until barely tender)*; stir in 3 T. olive oil. Add ½ C. pure maple syrup, 1 T. orange zest, and ½ tsp. cinnamon; stir to coat. Spritz a big piece of heavy-duty foil with cooking spray and dump the squash mixture onto the foil; top with 3 T. butter *(sliced)*. Wrap the foil around the squash, leaving a little space inside for air to circulate; seal edges tightly.

Set the foil pack on the grill, close the lid, and cook for 20 minutes, until tender. Open packet carefully and stir before serving.

Fettuccine Primavera

½ lb. fettuccine noodles

2 T. butter

3 C. very thinly sliced fresh veggies (we used bell pepper, carrots, and zucchini, but any combo will work)

3 C. heavy cream

⅔ C. frozen peas, thawed

Salt, black pepper, and cayenne pepper to taste

2 C. shredded Italian cheese blend

In a big skillet, cook the noodles according to package directions; drain, but reserve 1 cup of the cooking liquid.

In the same skillet over medium heat, melt the butter. Add the reserved cooking liquid and the fresh veggies; cover and cook over medium-low heat for a few minutes, until just tender. Add the cream, peas, salt, black pepper, and cayenne pepper; bring to a simmer. Toss the set-aside noodles with the veggies and add the cheese; simmer until the sauce thickens.

Serves 4

Balsamic Veggie Salad

1½ lbs. red potatoes, cubed

Salt

¾ lb. fresh green beans, trimmed & quartered

¼ C. chopped fresh basil

1 small red onion, chopped

1 tomato, diced

1 (2.25 oz.) can sliced black olives, drained

Black pepper to taste

¾ to 1 C. balsamic vinaigrette

Put the potatoes and 1 tablespoon salt into a big saucepan and add cold water to cover by 2". Cover and bring to a boil. Cook about 10 minutes or until the potatoes are just tender; transfer the potatoes to a big bowl to cool. Dump the beans into the cooking water and boil for 3 to 5 minutes; drain and plunge the beans into ice water.

When everything is cool, add the beans, basil, onion, tomato, and olives to the potatoes. Pour about half the vinaigrette over the salad and stir gently to coat; stir in as much of the remaining vinaigrette as you'd like; season with salt and black pepper. Chill several hours before serving.

Chili-Orange Chicken

¾ C. enchilada sauce

¼ C. BBQ sauce

1 tsp. salt, divided

1 T. chili powder

1 tsp. ground cumin

4 bone-in, skin-on chicken breast halves

⅓ C. orange marmalade

½ C. chopped cilantro

1 T. orange zest

In a big greased slow cooker mix the enchilada sauce, BBQ sauce, and ½ teaspoon of the salt. On a plate, mix the chili powder, cumin, and the remaining ½ teaspoon salt. Coat the chicken with the dry mixture and arrange in the cooker. Cover and cook on high for 2½ to 3 hours, until the internal temperature of the chicken reaches 165°.

Turn off the cooker; transfer the chicken to a serving plate. To the liquid in the cooker, stir in the marmalade, cilantro, and orange zest and serve over the chicken. **Serves 4**

Curry Chicken & Rice

Pour 1¾ C. water and 1 T. olive oil into a big saucepan and bring to a boil. Stir in 1 (7.2 oz.) pkg. rice pilaf mix and its seasonings; add 1 tsp. curry powder and return to a boil. Reduce the heat, cover, and simmer for 15 minutes.

Stir in 2 C. shredded cooked chicken, 1 (14.5 oz.) can diced tomatoes with green chiles, and 1 C. frozen peas. Cook, covered, for 8 to 10 minutes longer or until the liquid is nearly absorbed and the rice is tender. Toss on a handful of cashews before serving.

One Pot Lasagna

1 T. vegetable oil

1 lb. ground turkey

½ tsp. garlic powder

½ tsp. onion powder

½ tsp. red pepper flakes

Salt and black pepper to taste

6 oz. mini lasagna noodles (mafalda)

1 (24 oz.) jar marinara sauce

2 C. chicken stock

½ C. shredded mozzarella cheese

¼ C. grated Parmesan cheese

¾ C. cottage cheese

Heat the oil in a medium saucepan over medium-high heat. Add the ground turkey and cook until no longer pink, crumbling it while it cooks; drain and return to the saucepan.

Stir in the garlic powder, onion powder, pepper flakes, salt, and black pepper and cook for a minute or two. Stir in the noodles, marinara sauce, and stock. Bring to a boil, cover, and simmer for 20 minutes, until the noodles are tender, stirring often.

Remove the pan from the heat and stir in half the mozzarella and Parmesan cheeses. Drop the cottage cheese in blobs over the top and sprinkle with the remaining mozzarella and Parmesan. Cover and let stand off the heat until melted. Stir gently before serving.

Campfire Parmesan Corn

Spread a generous amount of softened butter over the entire surface of sweet corn *(as many ears as you need, husked & silk removed)*; sprinkle with grated Parmesan, dried rosemary, salt, and black pepper to taste.

Place the ears on a big piece of foil *(up to four ears per piece of foil)* and toss on a few ice cubes. Wrap the foil around the corn, leaving a little space inside for air to circulate; seal edges tightly. Place in hot coals for 20 minutes or until the corn is tender, turning the pack occasionally. Remove the pack from the fire using tongs and open carefully.

Sausage Skillet

1 T. olive oil

4 uncooked Italian sausage links

2 shallots, sliced

1 T. minced garlic

1 C. chicken broth

1 (15 oz.) can green beans, drained

1 (15 oz.) can cannellini beans, drained

8 oz. cherry tomatoes, halved

1 T. dried Italian seasoning

Salt and black pepper to taste

In a big skillet, heat the oil over medium heat. Add the sausage links and cook for 10 minutes, turning occasionally. Add the shallots and garlic and cook for 30 seconds. Pour in the broth and bring to a boil; reduce heat and simmer, covered, for 5 minutes. Add all the beans and return to a simmer. Cover and cook 5 minutes more or until sausage is done *(160˚)*.

Remove the skillet from the heat and stir in the tomatoes, Italian seasoning, salt, and black pepper.
Serves 4

Teriyaki Onion Burgers

1½ lbs. lean ground beef

About ½ C. teriyaki sauce, divided

1 (3 oz.) can French fried onions, crushed

6 hamburger buns, split

2 C. finely shredded green cabbage

Grease the grill grate and preheat the grill on high heat. Mix the ground beef, ¼ cup plus 2 tablespoons of the teriyaki sauce, and the French fried onions; shape into six patties.

Grill the patties for 5 minutes on each side or until done to your liking, brushing occasionally with the remaining 2 tablespoons teriyaki sauce. Spritz cut sides of buns with cooking spray and grill until toasted.

Serve burgers and cabbage on toasted buns.

Garlic Shrimp Tortellini

1 (19 oz.) pkg. frozen cheese tortellini

1 head broccoli, cut into small florets

¼ C. olive oil

12 oz. shrimp, peeled & deveined, partially thawed if frozen

2 T. minced garlic, divided

¼ C. butter

½ tsp. red pepper flakes

¼ C. flour

2 C. milk, plus more as needed

1 C. half & half

4 oz. cream cheese, cubed & softened

½ C. shredded Parmesan cheese

Salt and black pepper to taste

Cook the tortellini in a big saucepan according to package directions, adding the broccoli during the last 3 minutes of cooking time; drain and rinse with cool water and set aside.

Heat the now-empty pan over medium-high heat; add oil, shrimp, and 1 tablespoon of the garlic, cooking until shrimp turn pink, stirring occasionally. Transfer to a bowl and set aside.

Melt the butter in the empty pan over medium heat. Add the pepper flakes and the remaining 1 tablespoon garlic; cook about 30 seconds. Whisk in the flour until lightly browned. Gradually whisk in 2 cups milk and the half & half; cook for 6 to 8 minutes or until slightly thickened, whisking constantly. Stir in the cream cheese and Parmesan cheese, stirring until melted, adding a little more milk if the mixture is too thick. Season with salt and black pepper. Add the set-aside tortellini and broccoli and toss to combine.

Top each serving with the set-aside shrimp.

Cornbread Minis

Stir together 1 (8.5 oz.) pkg. corn muffin mix and the egg and milk called for on the muffin mix package; stir in ¼ C. shredded Pepper Jack cheese, 2 T. chopped canned chiles *(drained)*, and ¼ C. whole kernel corn *(drained)*.

Grease pie irons, fill with batter, and close; hold level above warm coals until both sides are brown, turning often. Serve with Chipotle Butter *(recipe below)*.
Makes 8

Chipotle Butter: Stir together 2 chipotle peppers in adobo *(chopped)*, ¼ C. soft butter, and 2 T. honey.

Breakfast Pizza

1 (8 oz.) tube refrigerated
   crescent roll dough

Garlic salt and black pepper to taste

½ lb. breakfast sausage

1 C. shredded hash browns, thawed

Salt to taste

1 C. shredded cheese (any kind)

A handful of sliced green onion

5 eggs

¼ C. milk

Hot sauce, optional

Heat oven to 375°. Line a
9 x 13" baking pan with foil; spritz
with cooking spray. Unroll the dough
and push it into the pan, pressing the
seams together and forming a ridge
around the edges; sprinkle with garlic
salt and black pepper and set aside.

Cook the sausage until no longer
pink, crumbling it as it cooks; drain
and scatter evenly over the dough.
Add the hash browns; season with
salt and black pepper. Top with the
cheese and green onion.

Beat the eggs with the milk and pour
evenly over the food; season with
garlic salt and black pepper. Bake for
20 minutes, until the eggs are set.
Drizzle with hot sauce. **Serves 6**

Fruit Parfaits

For each parfait, mix 1 (6 oz.) container yogurt *(any flavor)* with ¼ C. granola or quick-cooking oats and layer in a bowl or wide-mouth mason jar along with any add-ins* you choose *(mix and match what you love)*. Eat immediately or cover and chill up to 5 days.

* ***Add-in ideas:*** We used lemon yogurt with blackberries and graham cracker crumbs; coconut yogurt with pineapple chunks, sliced almonds and toasted coconut; raspberry yogurt with raspberries and raspberry jam.

Serves 4

Curry Up Kielbasa Skillet

2 T. olive oil

½ C. diced onion

2 sweet potatoes, peeled &
    diced into ½" pieces

1 Golden Delicious apple,
    diced into ½" pieces

1 (14 oz.) pkg. kielbasa, sliced

1 T. melted butter

½ tsp. curry powder

½ tsp. ground turmeric

½ tsp. chili powder

½ tsp. ground cumin

¼ tsp. ground coriander

¼ tsp. cinnamon

Preheat a heavy skillet over medium-high heat.

When the skillet is hot, add the oil, onion, and sweet potatoes and cook for 10 minutes. Meanwhile, in a bowl, mix the apple, kielbasa, butter, curry powder, turmeric, chili powder, cumin, coriander, and cinnamon.

Add the apple mixture to the skillet with the onion and sweet potatoes and cook 10 to 15 minutes longer, until the sweet potatoes are just tender. Give it a stir before serving.

Serves 4

Cranberry Chicken Fillets

In a bowl, stir together 1 C. dried sweetened cranberries, ½ C. apple juice, and ½ C. chicken stock; set aside. In a big zippered plastic bag, mix ¼ C. flour, ½ tsp. salt, and ½ tsp. black pepper. Cut 1 lb. boneless, skinless chicken breasts into ½" to ¾" strips; add to the bag, close, and shake to coat.

Cover the bottom of a medium skillet with vegetable oil and heat over medium-high heat. Add the coated chicken and cook until just golden brown on both sides, turning once *(they'll finish cooking later)*; transfer to a plate. Pour the set-aside cranberry mixture into the hot skillet, scraping up the browned bits. Stir in 1 T. Dijon mustard and decrease the heat to medium-low. Add the chicken and cook 8 to 10 minutes until done *(165˚)* and the sauce has thickened slightly.

Hot Hawaiian Sandwiches

About 18 slices deli ham

6 slices canned or fresh pineapple

2 T. Dijon mustard

1 T. honey

6 sweet Hawaiian rolls

6 slices cheddar or American cheese

Dry the ham and pineapple with paper towels. Stir together the mustard and honey. Split the rolls and spread some of the mustard mixture over the cut sides. On the bottom of each roll, layer ham, pineapple, cheese, and the top half of the roll.

Wrap each sandwich in heavy-duty foil, sealing the edges. Place the sandwiches over a warm cooking fire or on a preheated grill until the cheese melts and everything is hot. Serve any remaining mustard mixture alongside the sandwiches.
Makes 6

Easy Sausage & Chicken Stew

3 T. olive oil

5 mild bratwurst or sausage links, casings removed

1 onion, chopped

1 shallot, chopped

3 carrots, chopped

1 chicken breast, cooked & diced

5 red potatoes, cut into chunks

1 (15 oz.) can cannellini beans, drained & rinsed

1 (49 oz.) can chicken broth

¼ C. grated Parmesan cheese

1 tsp. dried thyme leaves

Salt and black pepper to taste

5 C. chopped fresh kale

3 T. flour

¾ C. cold water

In a big saucepan, heat the oil over medium heat. Slice the sausages and add them to the hot oil along with the onion and shallot and cook until the sausages are done, stirring occasionally. Add the carrots, chicken, potatoes, beans, broth, Parmesan, thyme, salt, and black pepper and simmer for 30 minutes, until everything is tender, stirring in the kale during the last 10 minutes.

In a small bowl, stir together the flour and water until smooth and stir into the stew until slightly thickened.

Spinach Artichoke Melts

Softened butter

½ tsp. minced garlic

1 T. flour

½ C. milk

1½ T. cream cheese spread

½ C. shredded mozzarella cheese

½ C. grated Parmesan cheese

½ tsp. red pepper flakes

½ tsp. black pepper

½ C. sour cream

1 (6.7 oz.) jar artichokes, drained & chopped

½ C. diced grilled chicken breast

½ C. frozen chopped spinach, thawed, drained & squeezed dry

6 slices sourdough bread

Melt 1 tablespoon butter in a medium saucepan over medium heat. Add the garlic and cook for 1 minute. Whisk in the flour to make a paste then cook another minute or so. Slowly add the milk, cooking and stirring for a minute or two, until slightly thickened. Add the cream cheese spread, the mozzarella and Paremsan cheeses, red pepper flakes, and black pepper; stir until the cheese melts. Stir in the sour cream until smooth. Finally, stir in the artichokes, chicken, and spinach; remove from the heat.

Heat a large skillet or griddle over medium-low heat. Meanwhile, spread a few tablespoons of the artichoke mixture over half the bread slices and top with the remaining bread slices; butter the outside of each slice and lay the sandwiches in the hot pan.

Cook until both sides are golden brown and the filling is hot, turning halfway through cooking.

Bacon Fudge

Line an 8 x 8" pan with foil; coat with cooking spray. Cook 1 lb. diced bacon; drain, cool, & crumble. In a saucepan, combine 16 oz. semisweet baking chocolate *(chopped)*, 1 (14 oz.) can sweetened condensed milk, ¼ C. butter, and ¼ C. heavy cream; cook over low heat, stirring until melted. Add 1 C. chopped toasted pecans and all but ¼ C. of the bacon to the chocolate; stir to combine. Spread into the prepped pan and sprinkle with the remaining bacon. Chill until firm before cutting into 1" squares. **Makes 64 bite-size pieces**

Because every trip needs chocolate.

Simple Spaghetti

1 lb. lean ground beef

1 onion, chopped

3 (8 oz.) cans tomato sauce

1½ C. water

1½ tsp. salt

¼ tsp. black pepper

¼ tsp. garlic powder

1¼ tsp. dried oregano

8 oz. uncooked spaghetti noodles

1 C. shredded cheddar or mozzarella cheese, plus more for serving

Cook the ground beef and onion in a saucepan until done, breaking it up as it cooks.

Stir in the tomato sauce, water, salt, black pepper, garlic powder, and oregano. Bring to a boil. Add the noodles and reduce the heat to a simmer, stirring to separate; cover tightly and cook for 25 to 30 minutes. Uncover and stir in 1 cup cheese.

Top each serving with extra cheese if you'd like.

Serves 4

Overnight Apple Pie Oatmeal

Coat a big slow cooker heavily with coconut oil. Core & dice 2 Gala apples and toss them into the cooker. Add 1½ C. coconut milk, 1½ C. water, 1 C. steel cut oats, 1 T. coconut oil, ¼ to ½ tsp. sea salt, and 1 tsp. vanilla. Stir to blend.

Cook on low for 5 to 7 hours, until the apples and oats are tender. Top servings with brown sugar, cinnamon, half & half or more coconut milk, honey and/or maple syrup, and a sprinkling of chopped walnuts and/or flaked or toasted coconut.

Citrus Veggie Pack

2 C. carrot sticks

6 C. broccoli florets

⅓ C. orange marmalade

½ tsp. salt

1 tsp. water

1 (11 oz.) can mandarin
  oranges, drained

¼ C. chopped cashews

Heat oven to 400° and spritz a
24" length of heavy-duty
foil with cooking spray. Dump the
carrots and broccoli onto the foil.
Add the marmalade and salt and
stir to blend; add the water. Wrap
the foil around the vegetables,
leaving a little space inside for air
to circulate; seal edges tightly.

Bake for 20 minutes or until the
veggies are crisp-tender. Carefully
open the pack and stir in the
oranges. Sprinkle with the cashews
before serving. **Serves 6 to 8**

Make it oven-free: *Grill with
the lid closed about 15 minutes,
rotating the packs several times.*

39

BBQ Pork Burgers

2 lbs. ground pork

1 tsp. ground ginger

½ C. chopped green onions

¼ tsp. ground allspice

Salt and black pepper to taste

BBQ sauce

6 pineapple rings

Butter

6 hamburger buns

Spinach leaves

6 slices deli ham

Dump the ground pork, ginger, green onions, allspice, salt, and black pepper into a bowl and mix until just combined. Form six large patties and press an indentation into the top of each.

Grease the grill grates and preheat the grill on medium heat. Toss the patties on the grill and brush with BBQ sauce; cook with the lid closed until brown on the bottom, then flip and brush with more BBQ sauce. Cook until the internal temperature of the meat reaches 160°; set aside for 5 minutes. In the meantime, toss the pineapple slices on the grate and heat until lightly browned, turning once. Butter the cut sides of the buns and grill until toasted.

Put the spinach, burgers, more BBQ sauce, a slice of ham, and a grilled pineapple slice between the grilled buns.

41

Hash Packs

1 (24 oz.) bag frozen O'Brien hash browns, thawed

1 (8 oz.) pkg. diced ham (about 1⅓ C.)

4 strips cooked & chopped thick-cut bacon

4 eggs

1 (8 oz.) can whole kernel corn, drained

1 (4 oz.) jar pimentos, drained

¼ C. diced green bell pepper

2 tsp. onion salt

1 tsp. black pepper

4 slices American cheese

Preheat your grill to medium heat. Cut open the top of the hash brown bag, keeping the potatoes inside. To the potatoes, add the ham, bacon, eggs, corn, pimentos, bell pepper, onion salt, and black pepper; stir.

Spritz four big pieces of heavy-duty foil with cooking spray and crimp the edges. Divide the hash brown mixture evenly among the foil. Wrap the foil around the food, leaving a little space inside; seal edges tightly. Place the packs on the grill with the lid closed about 15 minutes, until the eggs are cooked. Carefully open packs and add cheese. **Serves 4**

Makes 8

Skillet Oreo Rolls

Heat oven to 375° and grease a 10" cast iron skillet. In a bowl, stir together 4 oz. softened cream cheese, 1 T. sugar, and 6 crushed Oreo cookies. Remove the rolls as a whole from 1 (13 oz.) tube refrigerated cinnamon rolls (8 ct.) and unroll into a rectangle *(make sure to buy the kind that can be unrolled)*; set aside the frosting packet. Spread the cream cheese mixture evenly over the rectangle; reroll, cut into individual rolls, and arrange in the prepped skillet. Bake for 15 to 20 minutes, until done. Spread or drizzle the set-aside frosting over the top.

Make it oven-free: *Cook on low heat in a covered grill or cover the skillet and cook on a rack over a warm campfire, until the rolls are done and no longer doughy.*

43

Bacon-Wrapped Chicken Kabobs

⅔ C. brown sugar

2 T. chili powder

1¼ lbs. boneless skinless chicken breasts

1 lb. bacon strips

Heat oven to 350°. Line a rimmed baking sheet with foil and place a wire rack on top. Coat rack with cooking spray. Soak wooden skewers in water for 30 minutes or use side-by-side metal skewers.

Mix brown sugar and chili powder in a shallow bowl. Cut chicken into 1" cubes and cut bacon strips into thirds. Wrap one bacon piece around a chicken cube and coat in the brown sugar mixture; slide onto a skewer. Repeat with remaining bacon and chicken, putting four or five on each skewer.

Arrange skewers on prepared rack. Bake 30 to 35 minutes or until the chicken is done and the bacon is crisp.

Make it oven-free: *Preheat your grill to medium heat, cover grates with greased foil, and grill the meat skewers until the chicken is done and the bacon is crisp.*

Omelet B'fast Sandwiches

Heat oven to 350°. Split and toast 6 English muffins. Slather each cut side with garlic & herb or garden vegetable cream cheese spread.

Whisk 6 eggs with ⅓ C. milk or water and pour into a hot greased skillet; cook until the eggs are done. Divide the egg mixture evenly among the bottoms of the English muffins. Top each with a handful of shredded Pepper Jack cheese, a folded slice of black forest ham, a little chopped fresh spinach and green onion, and the top half of the English muffin. Wrap in foil and bake for 15 minutes or until the cheese melts.

Make it oven-free: *Toss the foil-wrapped sandwiches on the grate of a preheated grill, close the lid, and heat for 15 minutes or until the cheese melts.*

BBQ Ranch Wraps

1¼ lbs. chicken breast, cut into thin strips

½ C. BBQ sauce, divided

1 C. diced red bell pepper

1 C. corn kernels (thawed if frozen; drained if canned)

⅓ C. ranch dressing

1 T. apple cider vinegar

Lettuce leaves

6 whole grain flatbreads

In a skillet over medium heat, cook the chicken in ¼ cup BBQ sauce until the chicken is no longer pink inside; remove from the pan. Once cool, dice the chicken into a big bowl and stir in the bell pepper and corn.

In a small bowl, whisk together the ranch dressing, vinegar, and the remaining ¼ cup BBQ sauce. Drizzle half the dressing mixture over the chicken and toss to coat.

Line each flatbread with lettuce and divide the chicken mixture evenly along the center of each. Roll up to enclose the filling. Serve with the remaining ranch dressing mixture. **Makes 6**

47

Loaded Potato Salad

3 lbs. red-skinned potatoes

Salt

3 eggs

8 dill pickle spears, diced

3 celery ribs, sliced

½ medium red onion, chopped

⅔ C. mayo

2 T. stone-ground mustard

2½ T. apple cider vinegar

2 T. chopped fresh dill

Black pepper to taste

In a big saucepan, cook the potatoes in salted boiling water until just tender; drain and let cool.

In the meantime, put the eggs in a single layer in a saucepan and add water to cover by 1". Bring to a boil; cover, remove from the heat, and let stand 15 minutes. Drain off the hot water and fill the saucepan with cold water and ice; let stand until the eggs are cool. Peel under cold running water and set aside.

Cut the cooled potatoes into bite-size pieces and chop the eggs; dump into a big bowl along with the pickles, celery, and onion.

In a small bowl, stir together the mayo, mustard, vinegar, and dill; pour the mixture over the vegetables in the bowl. Season with salt and black pepper and mix gently to blend.

Garden Pasta Salad

Cook 2 C. garden rotini pasta in boiling water to al dente according to package directions; rinse in cold water and drain well.

Combine the cooked pasta, ½ C. diced bell pepper *(any color)*, a handful of sliced cherry tomatoes, and ¼ C. sliced Kalamata olives. Stir in enough Italian dressing to moisten.

Chill until serving time.
Serves 4

Easy Tomato-Crab Bisque

1 (14 oz.) can fire-roasted
  tomatoes

1 (6 oz.) can tomato paste

2 C. chicken broth

½ C. finely chopped celery

¼ C. finely chopped onion

6 T. butter

2 T. flour

2½ C. half & half

1 tsp. salt

¼ tsp. black pepper

Old Bay seasoning and/or
  cayenne pepper to taste,
  optional

12 oz. refrigerated chunk
  crabmeat, roughly chopped

2 T. chopped fresh basil

In a medium saucepan, combine the tomatoes, tomato paste, broth, celery, and onion. Cook over medium-high heat for 10 minutes or until the celery has softened, stirring occasionally; remove from the heat.

In a big saucepan, melt the butter over low heat; whisk in the flour and cook for 1 minute, stirring constantly. Slowly stir in the half & half. Stir in the tomato mixture, 1 cup at a time. Stir in the salt, black pepper, and Old Bay and/or cayenne if using.

Bring to a light boil over medium-high heat then reduce heat to low. Stir in the crabmeat and basil; cover and simmer for 30 minutes, stirring occasionally.

Pastrami & Rye Bread Salad

½ C. thinly sliced red onion

3 C. cubed light rye bread

1 lb. tomatoes, coarsely chopped

¼ tsp. salt

2 mini cucumbers, thinly sliced

2 celery ribs, sliced

2 (2 oz.) pkgs. sliced pastrami, chopped

¾ C. fresh basil, chopped

Caraway seed

Red wine vinaigrette

Soak onion in a bowl of cold water for 10 minutes; drain, pat dry, and set aside.

Toast the bread in a 450° oven or in a skillet on the stovetop until the edges are crisp and golden brown, turning as needed to brown all sides; set aside to cool.

In a big serving bowl, combine the tomatoes, salt, and cooled bread cubes; toss well. Add the cucumbers, celery, pastrami, basil, and set-aside onions; sprinkle with caraway seed and serve with vinaigrette. **Serves 4**

Serves 4

Santa Fe Burgers

Grease the grill grate and preheat the grill on medium-high heat. In a bowl, combine 1 lb. ground turkey, 1 C. shredded Mexican cheese blend, ¼ C. salsa, ¼ C. crushed tortilla chips, ¼ C. chopped green onion, 1 tsp. smoked chili powder, and ½ tsp. garlic salt; mix lightly, shape into four patties, and press an indentation in the top of each.

Grill until the internal temperature of the meat reaches 160˚, turning to brown both sides. During the last minute or two, spread butter on the cut sides of 4 Kaiser rolls and grill until lightly toasted. Serve burgers on toasted rolls with lettuce, tomato, red onion, and salsa.

Crumb-Topped Orange Muffins

2½ C. flour, divided

1 T. plus ½ C. sugar, divided

3½ tsp. baking powder, divided

Salt

1½ T. brown sugar

6 T. butter, melted & cooled slightly

1 T. orange zest

¾ C. orange juice

⅓ C. vegetable oil

1 egg, beaten

Heat oven to 400° and line 12 muffin cups with foil liners. For the topping, stir together ½ cup of the flour, 1 tablespoon of the sugar, ½ teaspoon of the baking powder, a pinch of salt, the brown sugar, and the butter; set aside.

In a big bowl, stir together ½ teaspoon salt, the orange zest, and the remaining 2 cups flour, ½ cup sugar, and 3 teaspoons baking powder. Stir in the orange juice, oil, and egg until just moistened *(batter will be thick and lumpy)*. Divide the batter evenly among the prepped muffin cups. Divide the set-aside topping mixture evenly over the batter.

Bake for 20 minutes or until a toothpick inserted in the center comes out nearly clean.

Apple Muffins: Decrease sugar to 1 T. plus ¼ C.; add 1 tsp. cinnamon and 1 C. finely chopped, peeled apple to the dry ingredients. Substitute apple juice for orange juice. Bake 18 to 22 minutes.

Summer Salad

In a serving bowl, combine 2 diced tomatoes, 1 diced cucumber, 2 peeled & diced avocados, and ¼ of a chopped red onion.

Drizzle with 3 to 4 T. lime vinaigrette and stir gently to coat. Season with salt and black pepper and stir again.

Before serving, top with a little crumbled feta cheese. **Serves 4**

Turkey Tacos *w/Mango Salsa*

4 green onions

2 mangoes, peeled & cubed

Juice of 2 limes

2 T. chili powder, divided

1½ pints cherry tomatoes, quartered, divided

Salt & black pepper to taste

2 T. olive oil

½ small summer squash, grated

2 tsp. ground cumin

1 lb. ground turkey sausage

½ C. vegetable juice (mild or spicy)

8 taco shells

Your favorite taco toppings

Chop the green onions, keeping the white and green parts separate; toss ⅔ of the onion greens into a bowl along with the mangos, lime juice, and 1 tablespoon of the chili powder. Stir in about ⅔ of the tomatoes. Season with salt and black pepper and set aside.

Heat the oil in a big skillet over medium-high heat. Add the squash, cumin, the remaining 1 tablespoon chili powder, the remaining tomatoes, and the whites of the onions. Cook for 3 minutes. Add the sausage and cook until brown, breaking it apart as it cooks. Add the remaining onion greens and the vegetable juice; cook for 5 to 10 minutes or until most of the liquid has cooked away. Meanwhile, warm the taco shells either in a 400° oven for 6 minutes or wrapped in a barely damp cloth and microwaved for a minute or so until steaming.

Fill the warm shells with the meat mixture, the mango salsa, and your favorite toppings.

Pulled Pork with Slaw

Place 2 lbs. pork tenderloin in a slow cooker; pour 1 (12 oz.) can root beer over the top. Cover and cook on low for 8 hours, until pork shreds easily. Meanwhile, mix 1¼ C. coleslaw dressing, 1 (14 oz.) pkg. shredded coleslaw mix, ½ each green and red bell pepper *(diced)*, ½ C. diced onion, and 3 T. chopped parsley; chill until serving time.

Shred the cooked pork; discard the juices. Stir 1 (18 oz.) bottle BBQ sauce into the shredded pork. Serve on buns topped with the slaw.

Vegetable Beef Soup

1 T. canola oil

1 lb. lean ground beef

1 C. chopped onion

1 tsp. Italian seasoning

2 tsp. garlic powder

½ tsp. black pepper

2 C. beef broth

1 (8 oz.) can tomato sauce

2 (15 oz.) cans mixed vegetables, partially drained

1 (15 oz.) can diced tomatoes with green chilies (don't drain)

In a medium saucepan, heat the oil over medium-high heat. Add the ground beef and onion. Cook until the meat is no longer pink, crumbling it as it cooks; drain and return to the pan. Add the Italian seasoning, garlic powder, black pepper, broth, tomato sauce, mixed vegetables, and tomatoes.

Bring to a boil then reduce heat and cover; simmer for 20 minutes, stirring occasionally. **Serves 6**

Chopped Salad
w/Jalapeño Dressing

¼ C. pickled jalapeños, finely chopped

¼ C. mayo

¼ C. ranch dressing or sour cream

2 T. chopped cilantro

1 T. lime juice

½ tsp. paprika

1 to 2 T. milk or half & half

1 (15 oz.) can yellow hominy, drained, rinsed & patted dry

Cayenne pepper to taste

4 C. chopped Romaine lettuce

Grape tomatoes, halved

1 C. rotisserie chicken or leftover cooked chicken

1 mango, peeled, seeded & sliced

1 avocado, peeled, seeded & sliced

1 bell pepper, any color, sliced

Queso fresco or feta cheese, crumbled

Pumpkin seeds (pepitas)

In a mason jar or other lidded container, combine the pickled jalapeños, mayo, ranch dressing or sour cream, cilantro, lime juice, and paprika. Pour in enough milk to reach the consistency you like. Cover, shake, and chill until serving time.

In a medium skillet, heat hominy over low heat until just beginning to brown, stirring occasionally; sprinkle with cayenne pepper.

On a big tray, arrange the lettuce, hominy, tomatoes, chicken, mango, avocado, and bell pepper. Serve the chilled dressing, queso fresco or feta, and pumpkin seeds alongside.

This is an easy, build-your-own meal and can be personalized to your taste.

Sweet Potato Chili

2 T. olive oil

1 large onion, diced

2 sweet potatoes,
   peeled & diced

2 tsp. minced garlic

2 T. chili powder

1 T. ground cumin

½ tsp. chipotle powder

2 tsp. salt

2⅔ C. water

1 (15 oz.) can black beans,
   drained & rinsed

1 (15 oz.) can crushed
   tomatoes

1 T. lime juice

Optional toppings: sour
   cream, avocado,
   shredded cheese

Heat the oil in a big skillet over medium-high heat. Add the onion and sweet potatoes and sauté until slightly softened, stirring often. Add the garlic, chili powder, cumin, chipotle powder, and salt; heat for 30 seconds, stirring constantly. Add the water and bring to a simmer.

Cover, reduce heat to maintain a gentle simmer, and cook for 10 minutes or until the sweet potatoes are tender.

Stir in the black beans, tomatoes, and lime juice; heat to simmering, stirring often. Cook to slightly reduce the liquid.

Serve with desired toppings.

Omit the cumin and chipotle powder for a less smoky flavor.

Chai Latte

In a small saucepan, combine 2 C. milk or almond milk, ¾ tsp. cinnamon, ¼ tsp. ground ginger, ⅛ tsp. ground cloves, and 3 T. maple syrup. Whisk to combine.

Heat over medium-high heat until the mixture is a nice warm drinking temperature, whisking occasionally.

Pour into mugs and top with whipped cream; sprinkle with cinnamon, ginger, and or cloves if you'd like. **Serves 2**

Index